These pages are intentionally left blank.
In other words, men know nothing about women.

Still wondering?

I know what you are thinking...

Everything

Nothing

Something

But...

Maybe...

Surely...

Definitely...

These pages are intentionally left blank.
In other words, Men know nothing about women.

Something?

Nothing

Goodness

Nothing

Absolutely

Clearly

Maybe

Not

These pages are intentionally left blank.
Men know nothing about women.

Nothing

Everything

Something

Little

Unicorns

Hope

Careful

These pages are intentionally left blank.
Men know nothing about women.

Everything

Something

Nothing

Seriously

Nothing

These pages are intentionally left blank.
Men know nothing about women.

Nothing

Nothing

Nothing

Something?

Nope

Nothing

Wondering?

Why?

Accept it

These pages are intentionally left blank.
Men know nothing about women.

Got It

Nothing!

Nothing

Already

Nothing

These pages are intentionally left blank.
Men know nothing about women.

Nothing.